Faunistics is a beautiful haiku collection that takes you on a worldwide trip of fauna. Both poems and illustrations make this book a complete poetic encyclopedia where one can find many aspects of wildlife ranging from the heights of the sky to the depths of the ocean. The simple but powerful illustrations add more meanings to the poems and make them more vivid, succinct, and thought-provoking. The wide range of poems will captivate readers to explore and unfold fauna in their surroundings or at least know about its significance. A must-read book that one can proudly put on their personal bookshelf.

Hifsa Ashraf, Author of *Hazy Crescent Moon* and
Touchstone Award Winner

Like an expert tour guide, Thomas whisks his readers from continent to continent, drawing our attention to an almost unmatched variety of international animal life. We get at times the beloved staples – tigers, giraffes, platypuses – but, intriguingly, we also get to see many of our world's lesser-known creatures, like New Zealand's kākāpōs, Brazil's nelore, or East Antarctica's nemerteans. And with skilful illustrations accompanying the poems along the way, *Faunistics* might just be the most engaging global roundtrip you'll ever take with haiku.

Aaron Barry, Co-Editor of *Prune Juice Journal*

Thomas' voice is both classical and refreshingly modern. His haiku draw the reader into the real wealth of our modern world: nature still pristine. His pen is established and playful. I roam in *the beetle's forest*. I read *the notes of singing dogs*. I watch how *the polar bear's jaw warms up*. This is a must-read for anyone who enjoys haiku of the natural world by a poet whose path I look forward to following.

Réka Nyitrai, Co-Author of *Barking at the Coming Rain* and
Touchstone Award Winner

R.C. Thomas' new collection is a veritable haiku bestiary. Sited in the natural world his poems are also engagingly modern in both style and compass. Thomas is never afraid to bend the genre to his own ends and the result is a fascinating, cliché-free collection. Already well-known for his longer verse, this first book of haiku amply showcases the depth of his often playful, always arresting vision. A bravura performance from start to finish. Highly recommended.

Alan Peat, Co-Author of *Barking at the Coming Rain* and Touchstone Award Winner

R.C. Thomas, an award-winning poet and member of the British Haiku Society, has produced a truly unique collection of haiku with rich and imaginative illustrations. The reader is taken on a wild adventure – the haiku peek through noses and ears, fly with feathers, swim with fins, and follow the trails of paws and hooves. An inimitable poetic atmosphere with different sounds and colours which highlight the special characteristics of the fauna on all continents. It's simply Faunistic!

Iliyana Stoyanova, Editor of *Blithe Spirit*

Faunistics is a collection of wild haiku and illustrations by R. C. Thomas using haikai *legerdemain*, and faunistic studies help prove the existence of creatures, sometimes by random sampling.

wind leaves the sound of the violin beetle's forest

Can haiku be close-up magic (*prestidigitation*) with nimble fingers: after all, Teijiro Ishida (Japan) invented the *Tenkai palm* for concealing and revealing, just as haiku poets do with pen, pencil, or mother keyboard.

not seeing the light dome land snail's low deepens

Jonah Weiner's *New York Times Magazine* 2017 profile on Derek DelGaudio reveals his art for spectators to become vitally and unpredictably indispensable in creating meaning, as R.C. Thomas does with his haiku, with creatures great, and small.

> winter moving
> moss spores
> on each millipede leg

Employ all your senses dear reader, as the author takes you on a mysteriously magical ride.

Alan Summers, Founder of *Call of the Page*

R.C. Thomas resides in Plymouth, UK. His poetry collections, The Strangest Thankyou (2012), and Zygote Poems (2015), were published by Cultured Llama under the name Richard Thomas, and his work has appeared internationally. He edited Symmetry Pebbles, was Creative Writing editor for Tribe, co-edited Thief, and was Managing Editor of INK, Plymouth University's creative writing journal. He was shortlisted for the Touchstone Awards for Individual Poems in 2022, received joint first place in the Sharpening the Green Pencil Haiku Contest 2022, first place in the Third Maya Lyubenova Haiku Contest, had a 'Selected Haiku Submission' in the 13th Yamadera Basho Memorial Museum English Haiku Contest, and was selected as one of the 'Top Creative Haiku Authors' in Europe in 2021 and 2022 consecutively.

Web: rcthomasthings.com
Etsy: etsy.com/uk/shop/RCThomasThings
Social: rcthomasthings

SCAN ME FOR ALL LINKS

ALSO BY R.C. THOMAS

The Strangest Thankyou (Richard Thomas)
Zygote Poems (Richard Thomas)

FAUNISTICS

A COLLECTION OF WILD
HAIKU AND ILLUSTRATIONS

R.C. THOMAS

First edition published in 2024 by R.C. Thomas Things

A CIP record for this book is available from The British Library

ISBN 978-1-3999-6873-7

Cover design and layout by R.C. Thomas

www.rcthomasthings.com

For fur thick with fresh dung, sticks and thorns; for feathers fanning the clouds along; for scales slick with wet earth; for beaks mining riches; for snouts snuffling for the sun between the trees; for trunks casting antennas; for muzzles and noses moist with the suspicion of food on the horizon; for paws amongst the dark, crumbling bark; for claws deep in the flesh; for hooves kicking up their dusty carpet; for fins folding the fossil juice; for the hundreds of millions of wild years that hang over the heads of the newcoming human who needs cutlery to eat, a plane to fly, chlorine to swim, shoes to walk, a park to swing, a sofa to sit, a toilet to shit.

CONTENTS

INTRODUCTION

This book was designed to simulate an around-the-world trip (so to speak; whether you return from the callous mountains of Antarctica is up to you). Regarding my selection of fauna and the countries this book visits, there was a lot of each to choose from, so I can guarantee that a lot have been missed, as a never-ending book didn't feel like a biologically-sound plan for either of us. Instead, I considered a mix of different fauna types, a balance of household names and those lesser-known, and fauna that would transport you to as many countries as possible, the final route decided on by which countries had fauna that was native, in its highest population, or the country was just well known for. You'll find fauna here that are in healthy supply as well those that are not, fauna that has just arrived and fauna that left a long time ago. You'll also find fauna that isn't technically 'wild' but they kept their place in this book on the basis that even the most domesticated fauna possess a wild heart. So, as for the inevitable missing fauna, and those asking, 'Where's the otter?', 'What about the skunk?' or, 'How have you forgotten the blue-bearded helmetcrest?': well, along with dozens of others, they came, ate, defecated all over my living room, and fled back into the wild. As for your own journey into the wild: bon voyage, safe travels, and enjoy your trip.

R.C. Thomas

EUROPE

spring rain...
freshwater flatworms
escape the downpour

between flowers
the red admiral
holding back

1

white wheat heads sway
the farm cat's
long whiskers

sundown
through every cell
queen bee's battle cry

slowly finding
the widest hole...
crow's sluggish earthworm

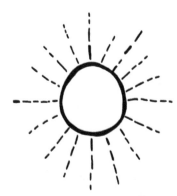

autumn sun
alighting from the gables
a city fox

lightning flash—
the lace web spider
covers its meal

silver lining—
what the storm takes
from the magpie's fable

UNITED KINGDOM

unearthing acorns
squirrel's winter
blowing over

Nordic giant
a tired lemming nurses
its cold foot

future histories in snow prints Iberian lynx

vineyard movement...
crescendos
of apollo butterflies

snow
not grass yet
early Alpine marmots

sensing a shift
blind mole rats let in
a little light

not seeing the **light dome land snail's low deepens**

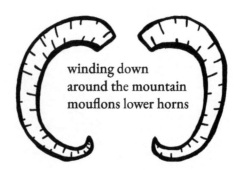

winding down
around the mountain
mouflons lower horns

further back Sicilian wolves' parallax ending

sun glitter
dispersing
sardines

stone rubbing
the Zingel asper makes
a body of work

blinking sun...
a wall lizard's
stop motion

AFRICA

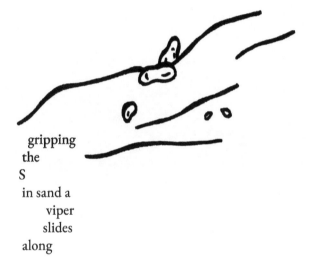

gripping
the
S
in sand a
viper
slides
along

deep within the green monkey gathering papayas

upon the river
one last star
the pygmy hippo sinks

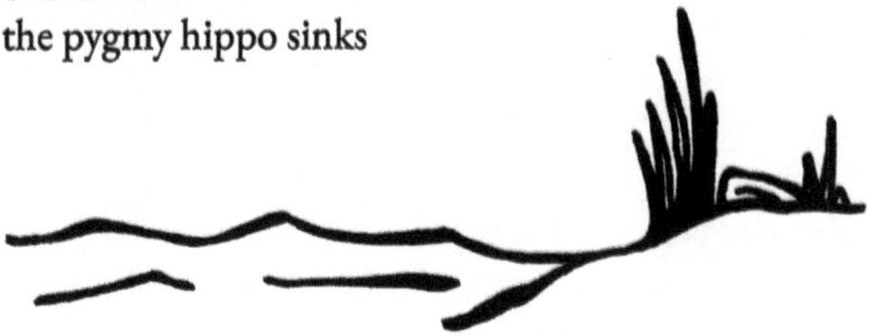

diamond moon...
brown hyenas sift
the gym dunes

parched for days
rhinos dwell upon
a watering hole

moonlighting
the aardvark's
night time construction work

seasonal depression...
the cape sand frog
buries its head

late summer's breeze
quickening its pace
an ostrich

seeing in the night
with its upside down
plain squeaker

plain painting
a lion's pride displays
its most vibrant mane

petrichor
from felled baobabs
b.nana emerges

new display—
the shoe box fate
of a dodo's skin

fallen star grass the elephant dreams on

following trail cracks—
the crooked necks
of giraffes

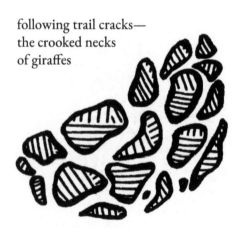

first impressions...
the meat stench
of a cheetah's breath

beating thunder—
a silverback claims
the berries first

mud tremors
the zebra foal
breaking in its hooves

finding itself
at a midpoint
a zorse looks back

catfish
ending a dry spell
the shoebill bows

calling it a day
dung beetles watch their sun
roll down again

ASIA

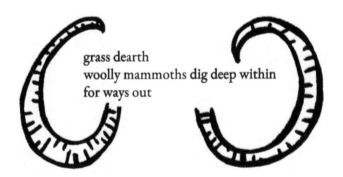

grass dearth
woolly mammoths dig deep within
for ways out

cake top evening
macaques huddle
with frosting

same rock
different river
silver carp wake

thawing out
the tree in the stream—
panda's late winter piss

revealing itself
crackling
dry leaves
king cobra sheds

new day
the tiger's darkest streak
brightens

grabbing a branch
the wind picks up
a black kite

slum hush...
not even a leopard's
soft paws through the dust

MALDIVES

caught in a vortex—
manta ray's flap
over plankton

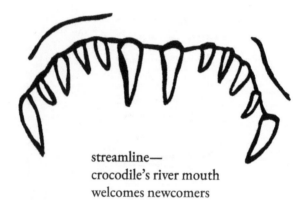

streamline—
crocodile's river mouth
welcomes newcomers

a breeze
through the long grass
white tips of goats' ears

refresh:
cave
angel
fish
step
out
of
their
pool

as far as the notion
of unicorns goes
saola range

deepening wound
the chevrotain holds onto
a grudge

wind leaves the sound of the violin beetle's forest

blood flow—
the water monitor's
oaring tongue

night sky of leaves
an orangutan makes
its bed

under the moon's weight
a slow loris steadies
its branch

babirusa
on its tusks
a puddle's perspective

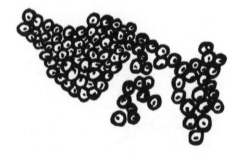

making life a mouthful Banggai cardinalfish

OCEANIA

howling wind...
notes of singing dogs
climb the mountains

morning cats!
Choiseul pigeon's
final wake-up call

passing
through
the
dark
cassowary
plum
seed
tree

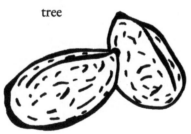

disappearing
with the earth
bilby burrows

the flow and
        the ebb and
        the duck of
the platypus

spawning coral
all around
a hammerhead's pan

sea growth—
an algae raft
for baby turtle

dogged—
the beached dingo's case
for driftwood bones

gaining ground at dusk
the shadiness
of male wombats

opposing thumbs a koala stands up for itself

becoming earth becoming air a kangaroo's bind

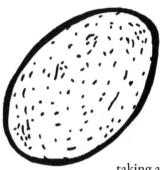

taking an egg
beneath its wing
emu's growing shadow

breaking clouds
a quokka laps
the water

electric night—
echidna knowing
the beetle's black

Tasmanian devil
the forest screams
now its found its wings

bringing light to forest floors sleeping kākāpōs fall

Proxima Centauri light hiding tuatara's third eye

reflecting on its tree climbing tree weta

forest clearing...
a kiwi's sneeze
blows away the cobwebs

new firefly wings...
the cosmos
beyond a glow worm

NORTH
AMERICA

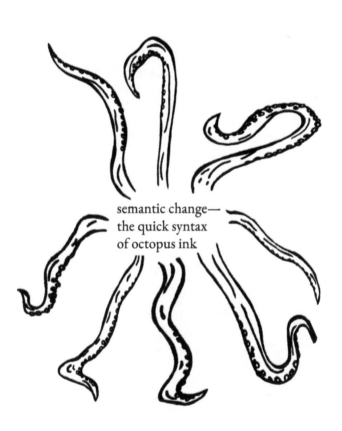

semantic change—
the quick syntax
of octopus ink

coaxing river—
black bears shadow
the wetted bound

hunting snow
a polar bear's jaw
warms up

last snow...
the spring
in a wolverine's gallop

a wood frog
thaws
the last brown fern

feeding time...
room for more
at Mother Coyote Inn

bullfrog...
the pond it's made
full of feathers

the old ways of rocks
eelgrass limpets
cling to their past

quietly moving snow
upon the branches
spirit moose

covering up the jellyfish light swarming lobsters

how the birch leans
in winter
beaver teeth graze

porcupine season—
a thinning spruce
grows new twigs

part of the parsley parsley worms eat parsley leaves

taking turns
with the earth
barracudas swim alone

every journey a song a dolphin clicks

winter moving
moss spores
on each millipede leg

drought
on the horizon 
longhorns licking up dew

volcano
rabbit
on
the
verge
of
historic
ash

opossum's faint visions of wild dogs playing dead

hour after hour the sun sets shark dials in circles

SOUTH
AMERICA

thunderheads...
the oilbird in the bucket
measures its fate

rain song...
the vibrato of tree frogs
loosening

squeezing out
every last detail...
anaconda's muscle memory

sun jumping stick to jumping stick

ecosystem—
a sloth hangs on
its every breath

taunting a marine iguana's belly flopping algae

darkness wetness the sea lion's feel for it

rock bottom...
piles of nurse sharks
for the shrimp

erasing grey clouds leaking pink flamingos

mountain clouds
tarucas pursue
their dreams

BOLIVIA

anteater's tongue
as long as day
the beckoned night

taking a branch and turning it emerald tree boa

white-faced saki...
the forest exposed
in the moon's image

dorados predict a fig dropping fish

dropping fish piranhas thank the fig

blowing free—
the nelore hide
in the open pasture

farewell summer—
young armadillo
packs up itself

caiman eyes...
jaguar losing its gaze
in the river

ARGENTINA

sun and sky
sewn together
a macaw drapes its wings

hippidion pool—
all the wet hooves
yet to come

dust clouds
Criollos lose
the moon again

ANTARCTICA

daybreak
dawning on the achromic
yellow king penguin

skimming trouble...
a gentoo penguin's
decline to sink

high ambitions...
chinstrap penguins
build upon their nest

squid!
white-winged albatrosses
test their buoyancy

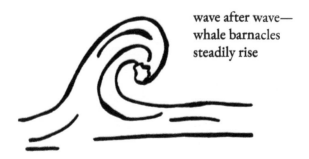

wave after wave—
whale barnacles
steadily rise

sperm whale rattles
the search for
colossal squid beaks

Thánatos
slipping
further
into
the
dark
nemerteans

hiding
glass sponge skeletons—
closet sea

life in the brinicle
winter casts
invertebrates

blubber markings...
the drop zones
of snow

finding clarity
in icefish
the ocean's see-through

just snow petrels before that nothing

a snowflake
for a moment
Antarctic midge

wave cycles
for every star
the same salp

glacial erratic—
a humpback whale
scours the ice floe

not a ripple
a seal pup bobs
in the ice crack

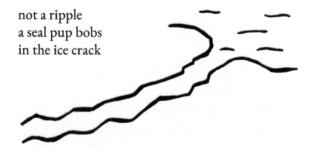

close enough arachnids sea spiders long to be

king tide—
Antarctic toothfish
begin to crown

sleeping through
snow rolling around
the sledge dog

polar days
in flora's place
Antarctosuchus remains

ACKNOWLEDGEMENTS

Thanks to the haikai community for their interest in and support of my short-form work. Thanks to my daughter Emmeline who has shown a loving interest in this work since the start and whose curiosity and Nat Geo Kids subscription has helped drive this project towards completion.

Quite a lot of these poems previously appeared in print and online publications: Akitsu Quarterly, The Asahi Shimbun, The Bamboo Hut, Blithe Spirit, Bloo Outlier, Bottlerockets, Cattails, Charlotte Digregorio's Writer's Blog, Cold Moon Journal, Creatrix, Dawn Returns: Haiku Society of America Anthology 2022 (ed. John J. Han), Die Leere Mitte, Fevers of the Mind, Fireflies' Light, Frameless Sky, Haiku Commentary, The Haiku Foundation's 'Haiku Dialogue', Heliosparrow, The Heron's Nest, Kokako, Kontinuum, Literary Revelations, Lothlorien Poetry Journal, The Mamba, Modern Haiku, the Nick Virgilio Haiku Association's 'Haiku in Action', NOON (Journal of the Short Poem), NZPS 2022 Anthology (ed. Tim Jones), Ourselves in Rivers and Oceans Anthology (ed. Claire Thom), Pages Literary Journal, The Pan Haiku Review, Rip-Roaring Haiku Anthology (ed. Corine Timmer), Scarlet Dragonfly Journal, Shadow Pond, Shamrock, Spillwords, Taj Mahal Review, Temple: The British Haiku Society's Anthology 2021 (ed. Iliyana Stoyanova), Time Haiku, Trash Panda, Treveni Haikai, tsuri-dōrō, Ubu., Under the Basho, and Wales Haiku Journal.

'skimming trouble...', 'squid!', 'finding clarity', 'wave cycles', and 'plain painting' were included in the Plymouth Art Vending Machine.

'calling it a day' was a 'Selected Haiku Submission' in the 13th Yamadera Basho Memorial Museum English Haiku Contest.

'silver lining—' won joint first place in the Sharpening the Green Pencil Haiku Contest 2022, and was shortlisted for the Touchstone Awards for Best Individual Poems 2022.

HEY READER

You made it to the end of the book. For that, I'm entirely grateful. Now you've come this far, could I ask for just one more thing? Would you consider leaving a review on Amazon, Goodreads, or wherever else you like to review books? Perhaps you could take a screenshot of your review and send it to me, and/or take a photo of yourself and the book and tag me in a social media post or story? All of this really helps a poet out (we're a struggling breed). In return, I'll send you a discount code to use in my shop: rcthomasthings.com.

Email: hi@rcthomasthings.com
Socials: rcthomasthings

Printed in Poland
by Amazon Fulfillment
Poland Sp. z o.o., Wrocław

31294252R30087